ANIMALS
Of The Forest

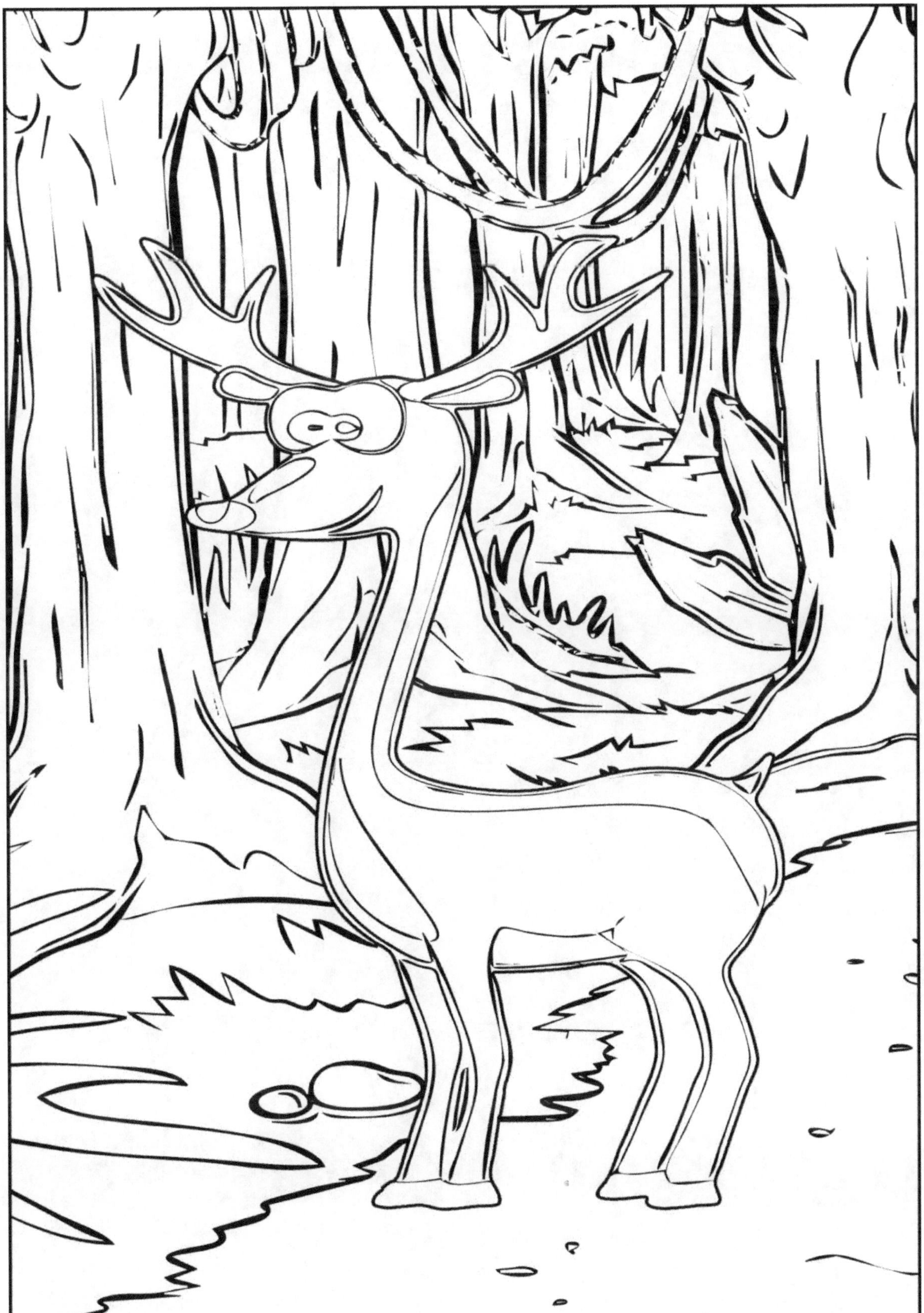

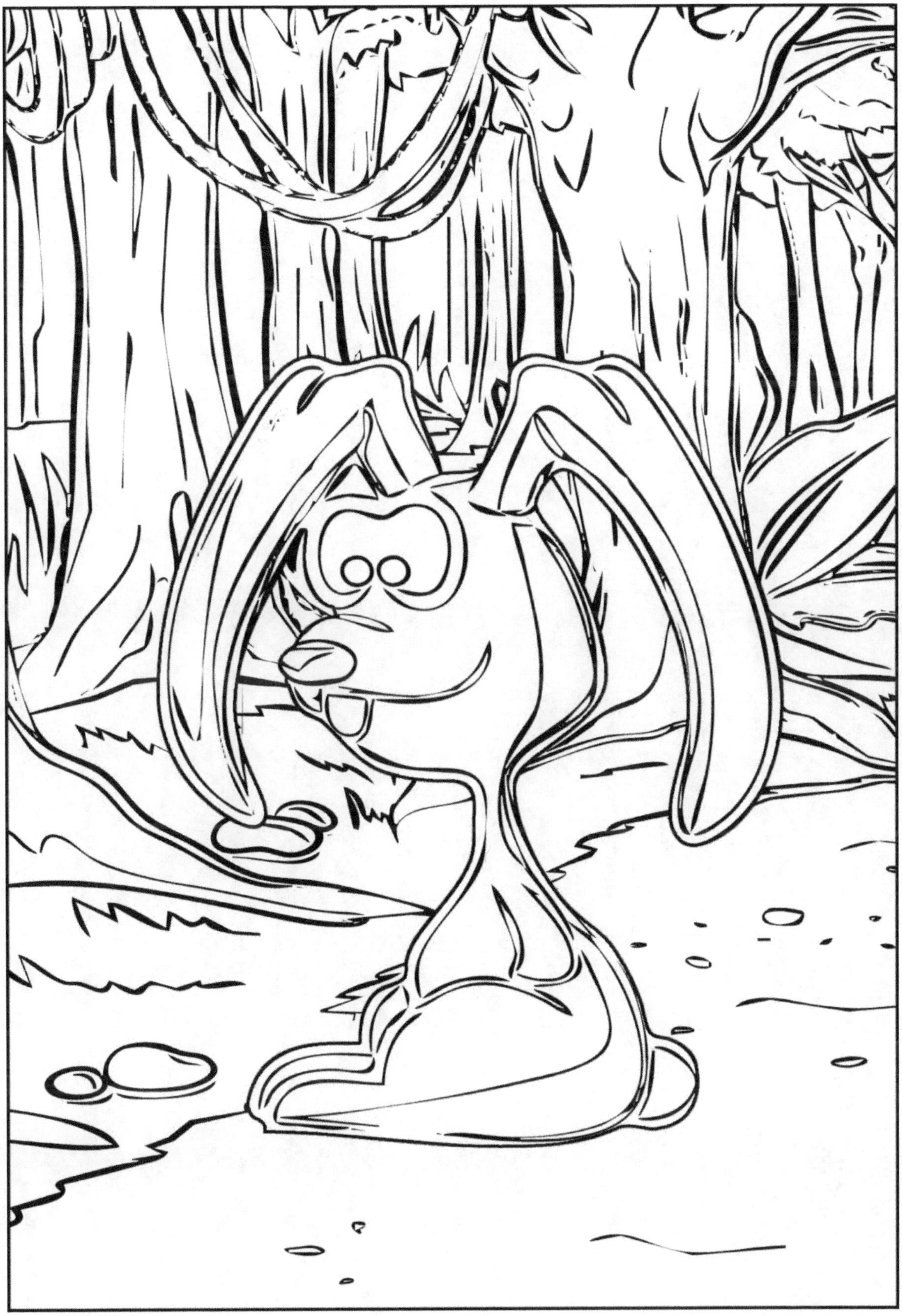

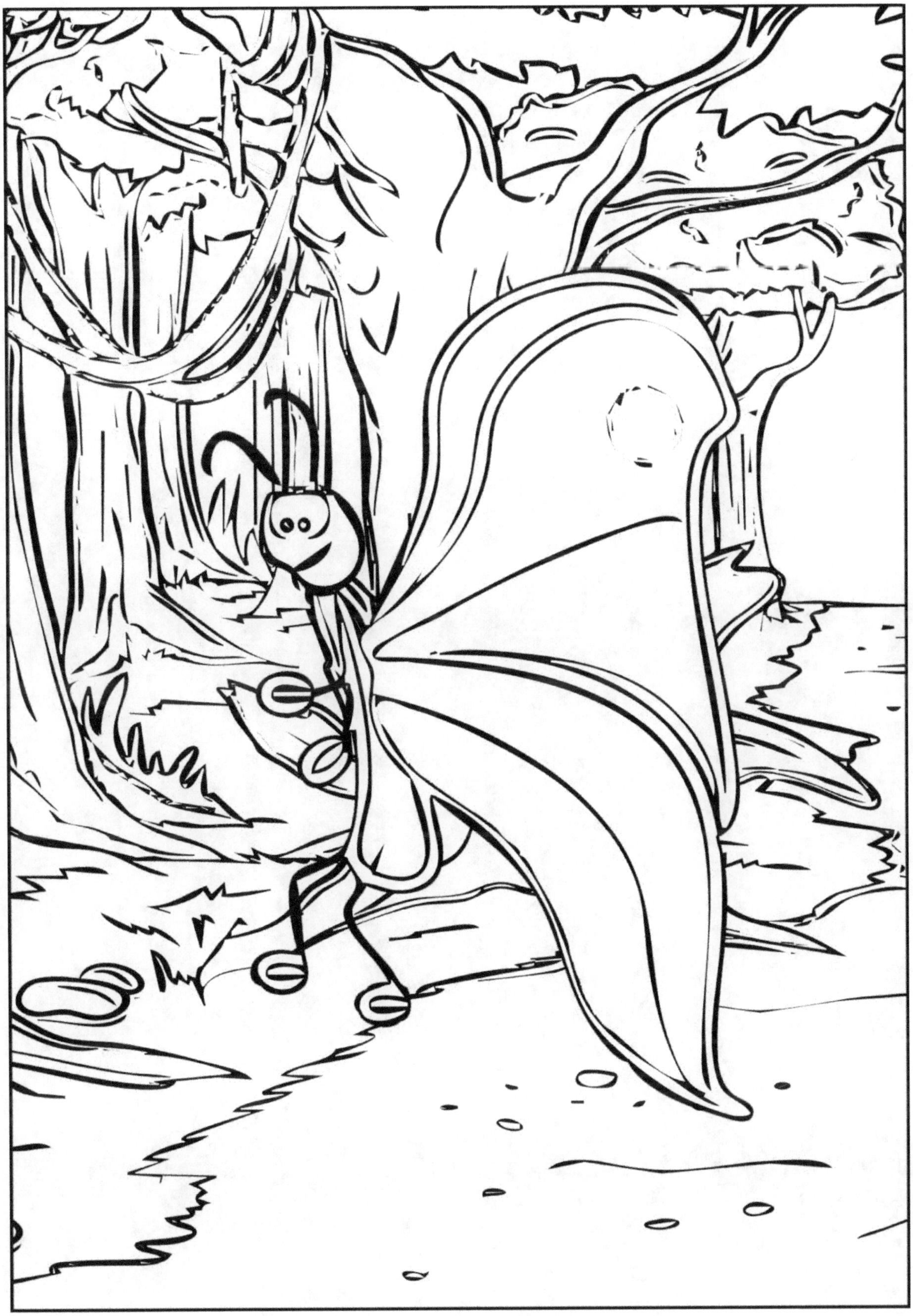

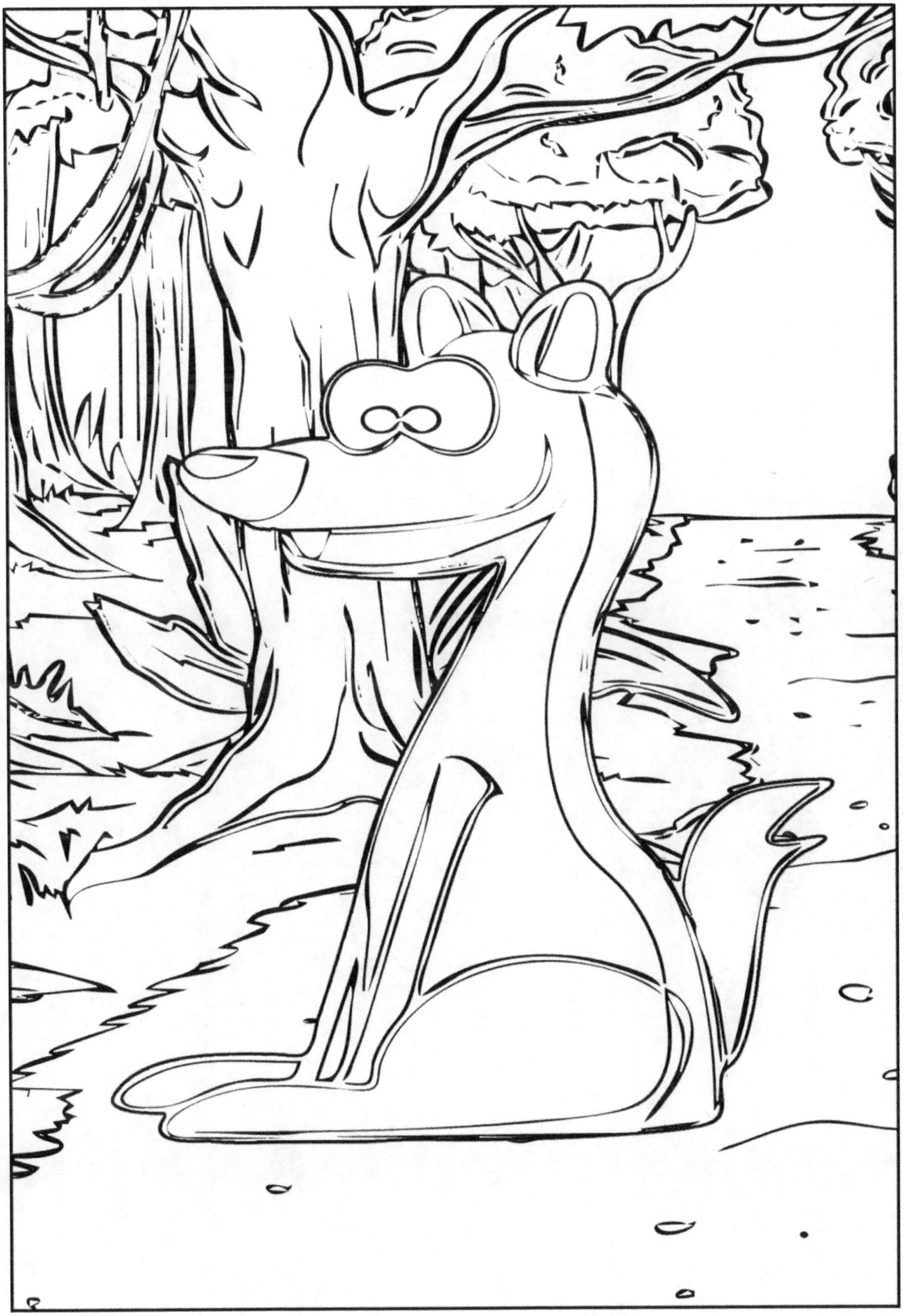

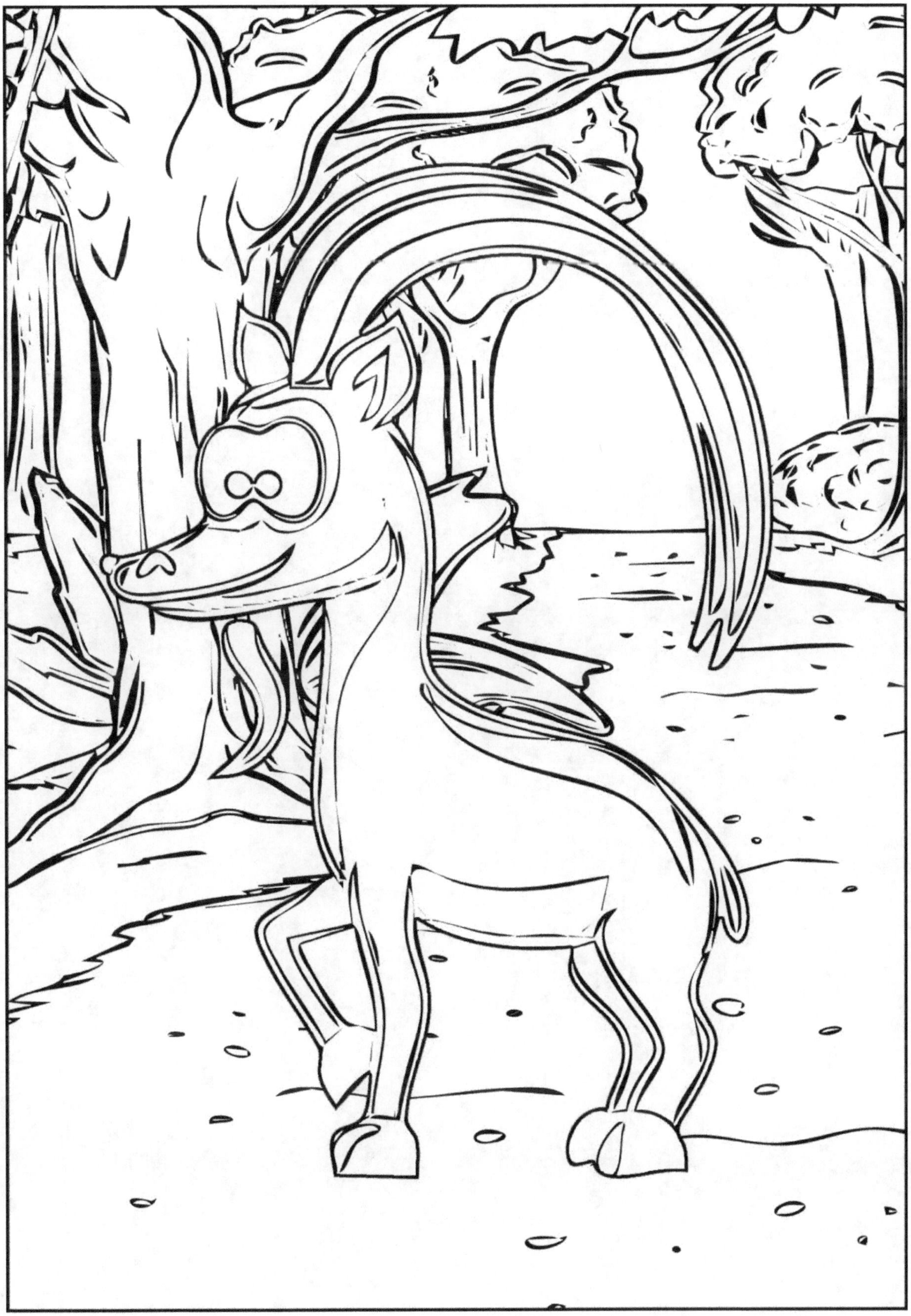

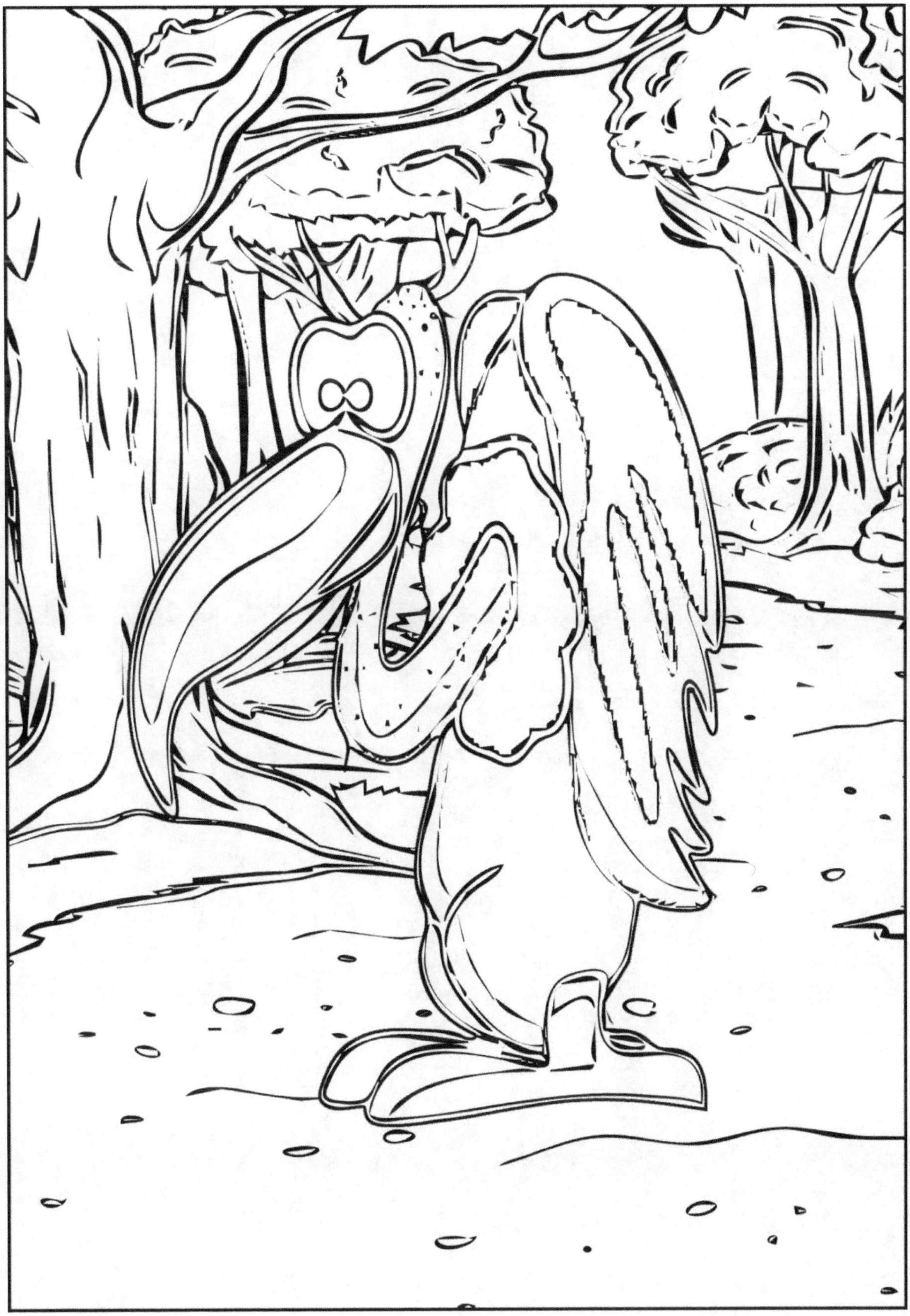

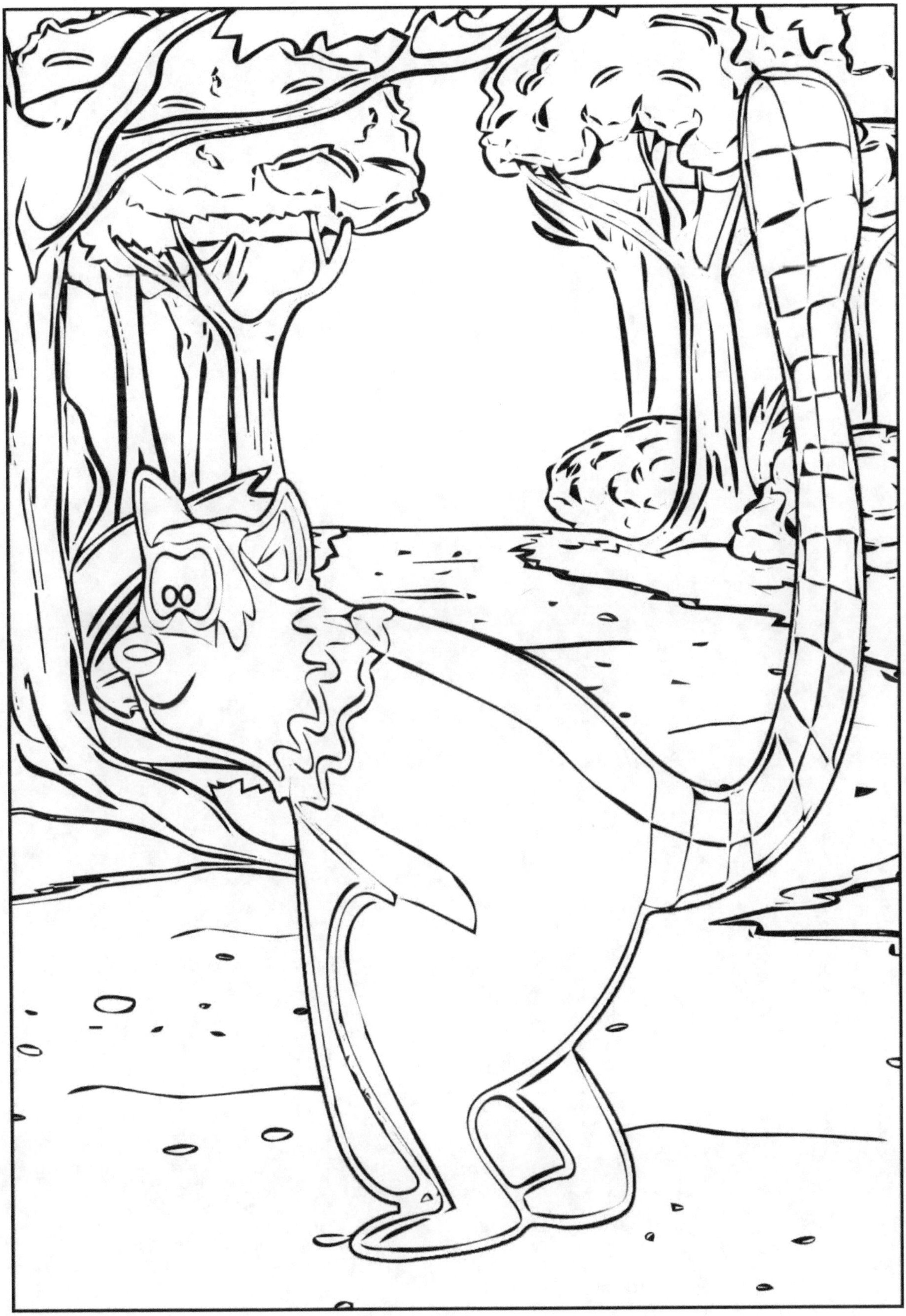

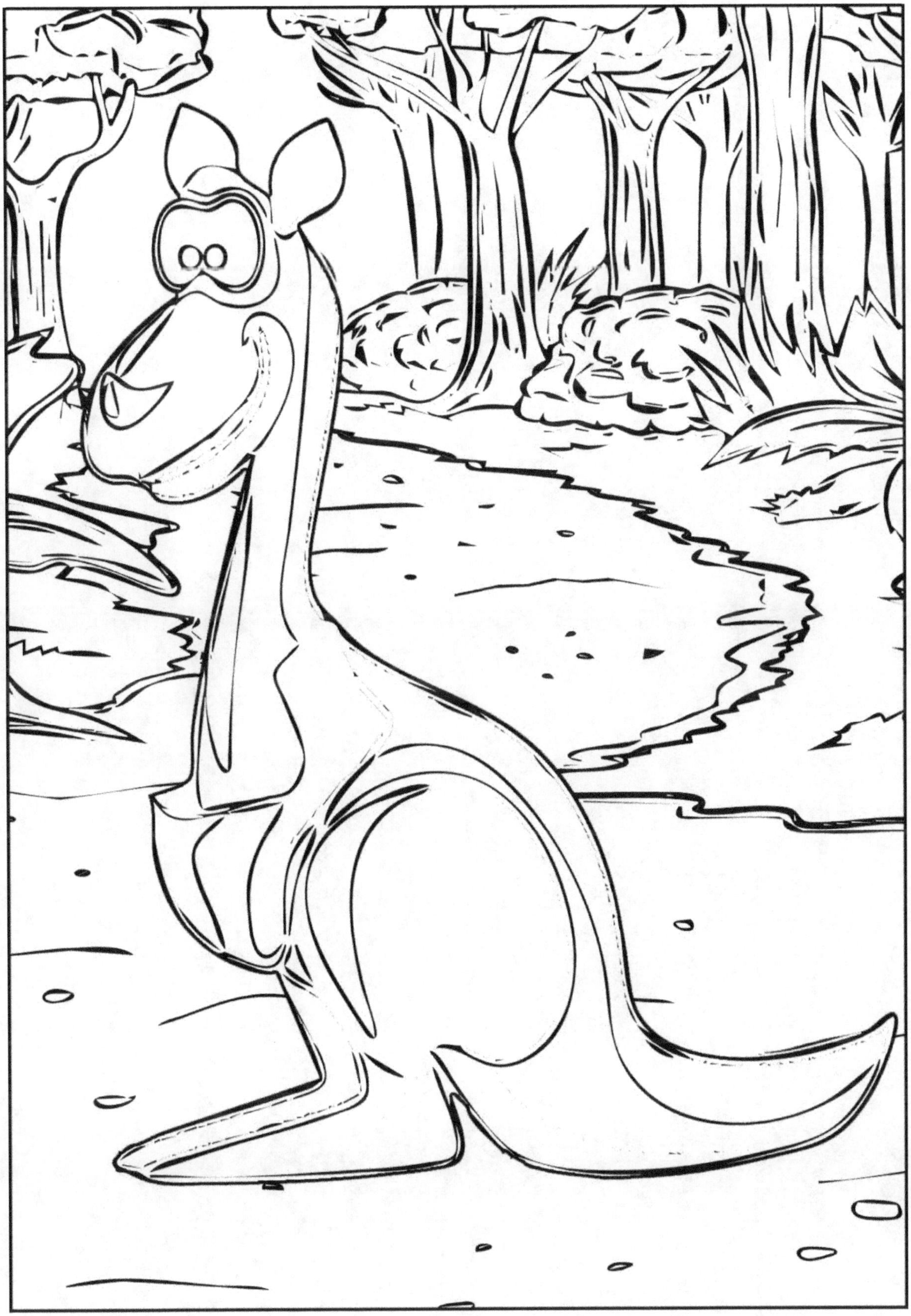

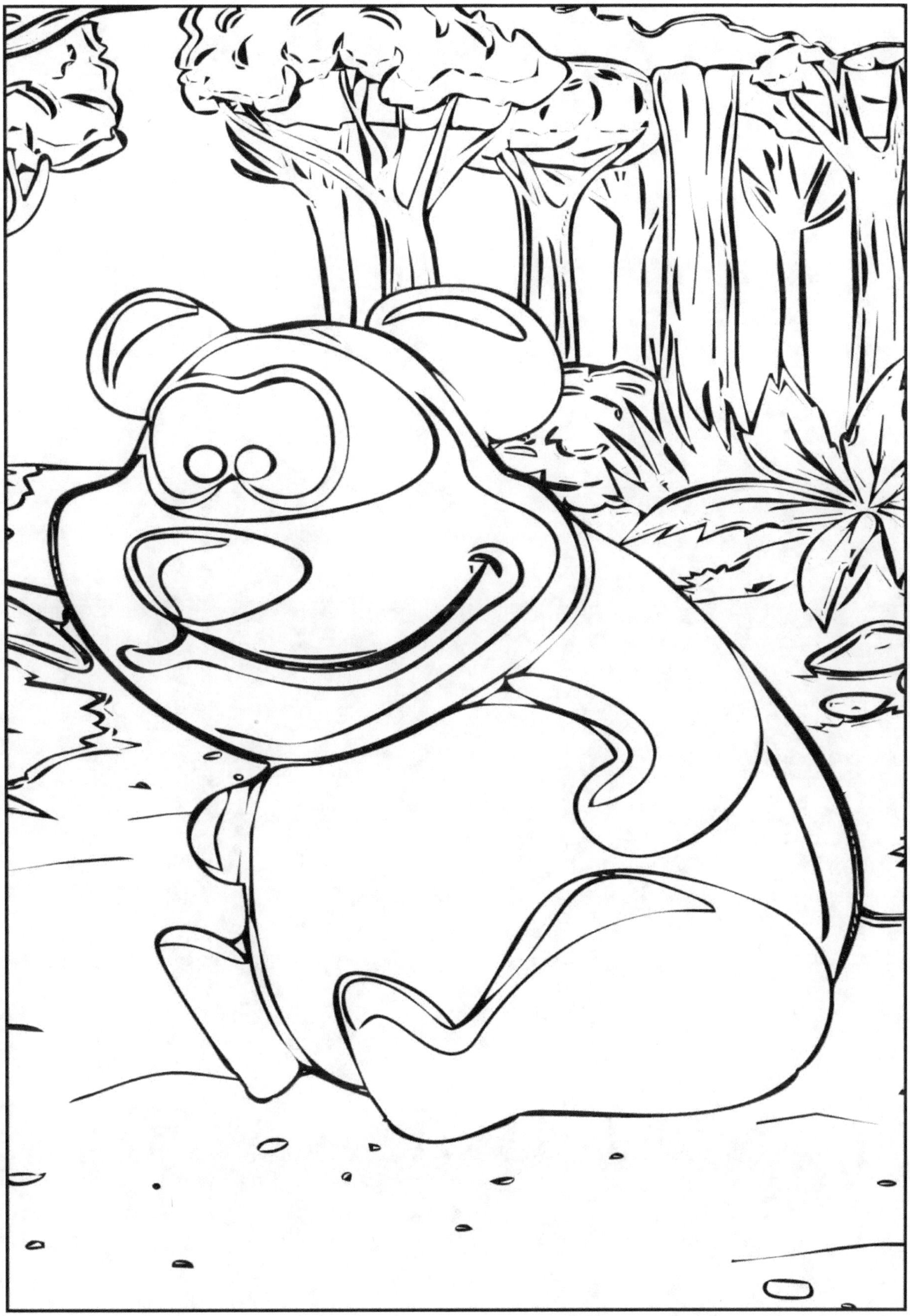

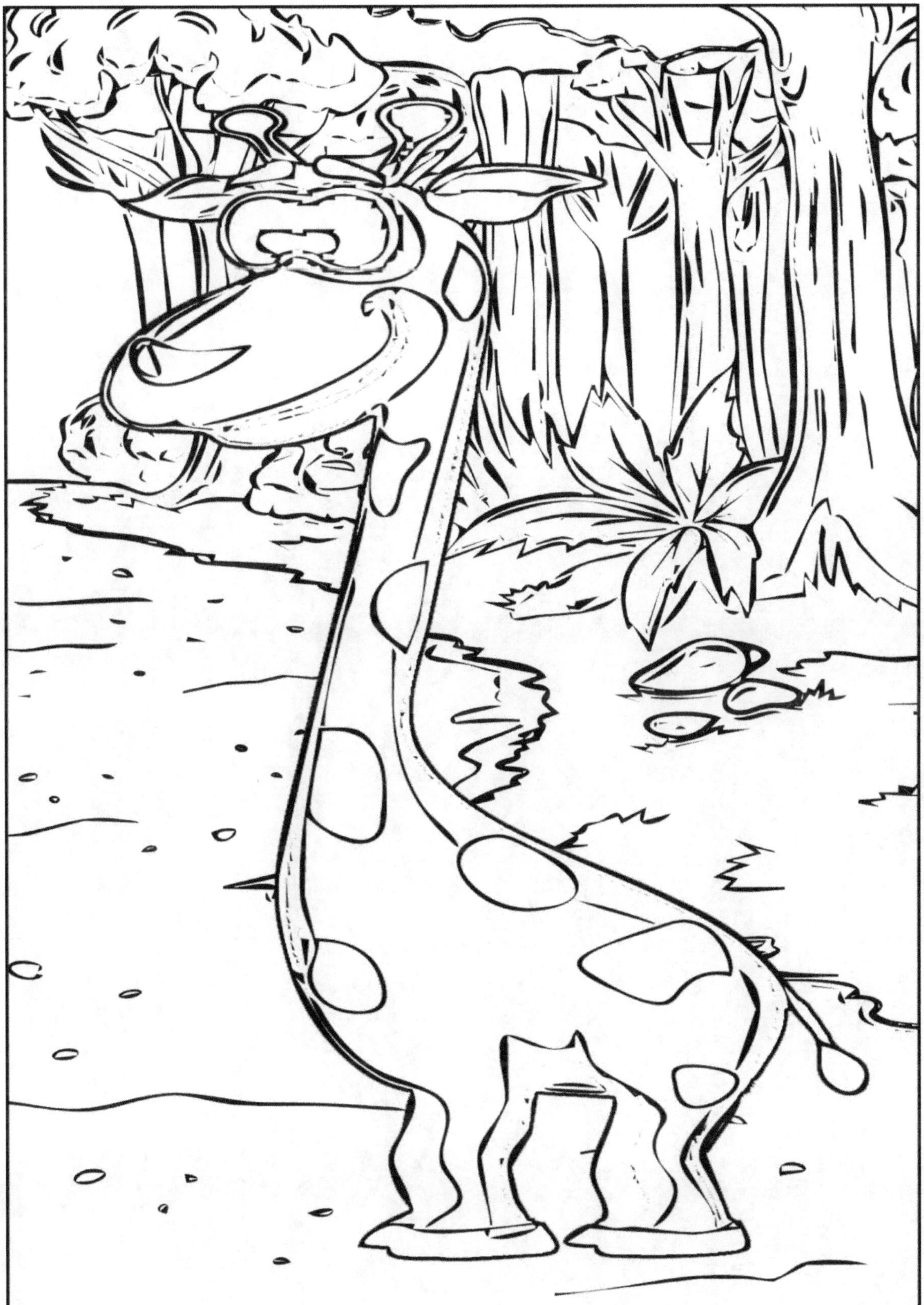

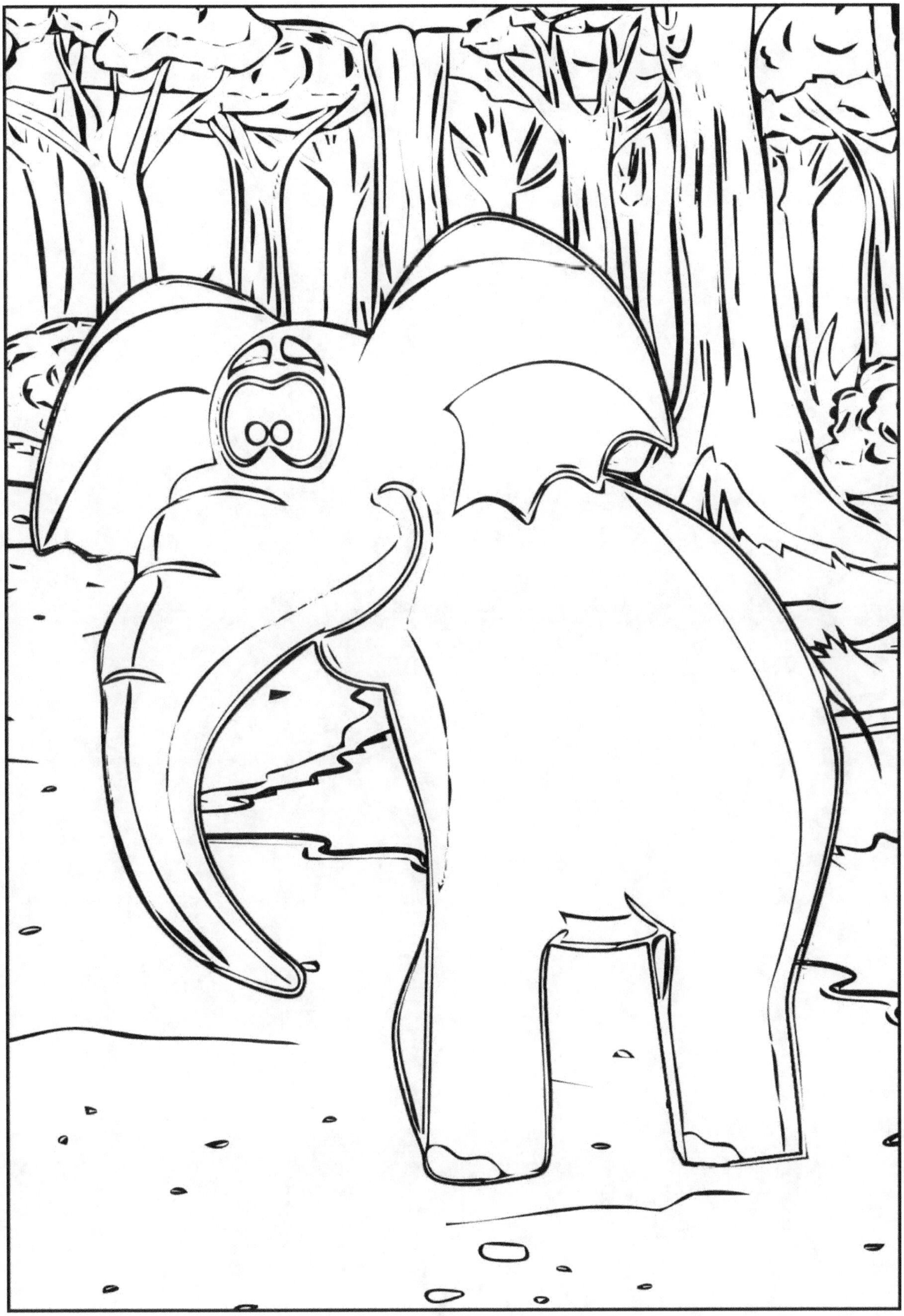

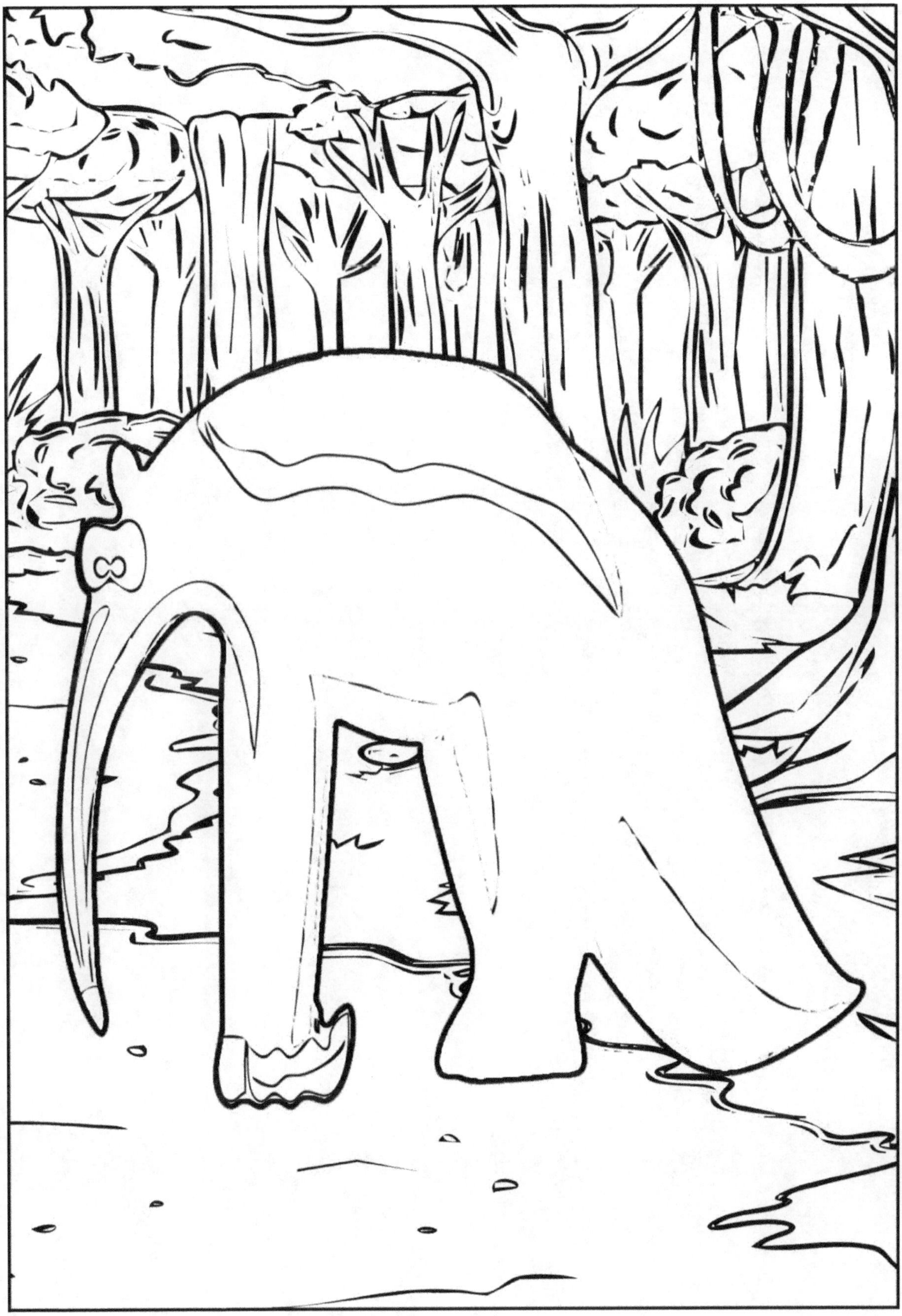

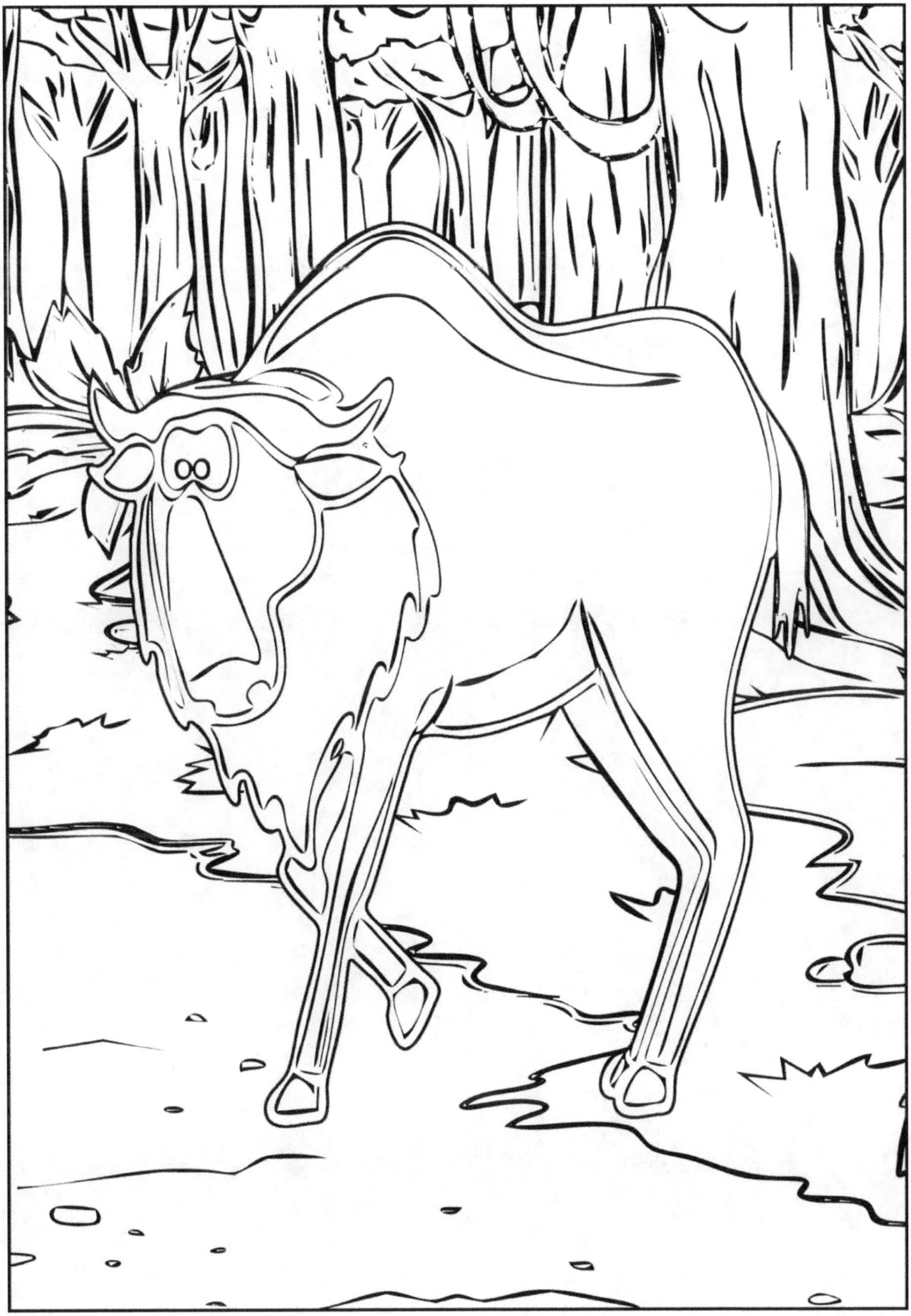

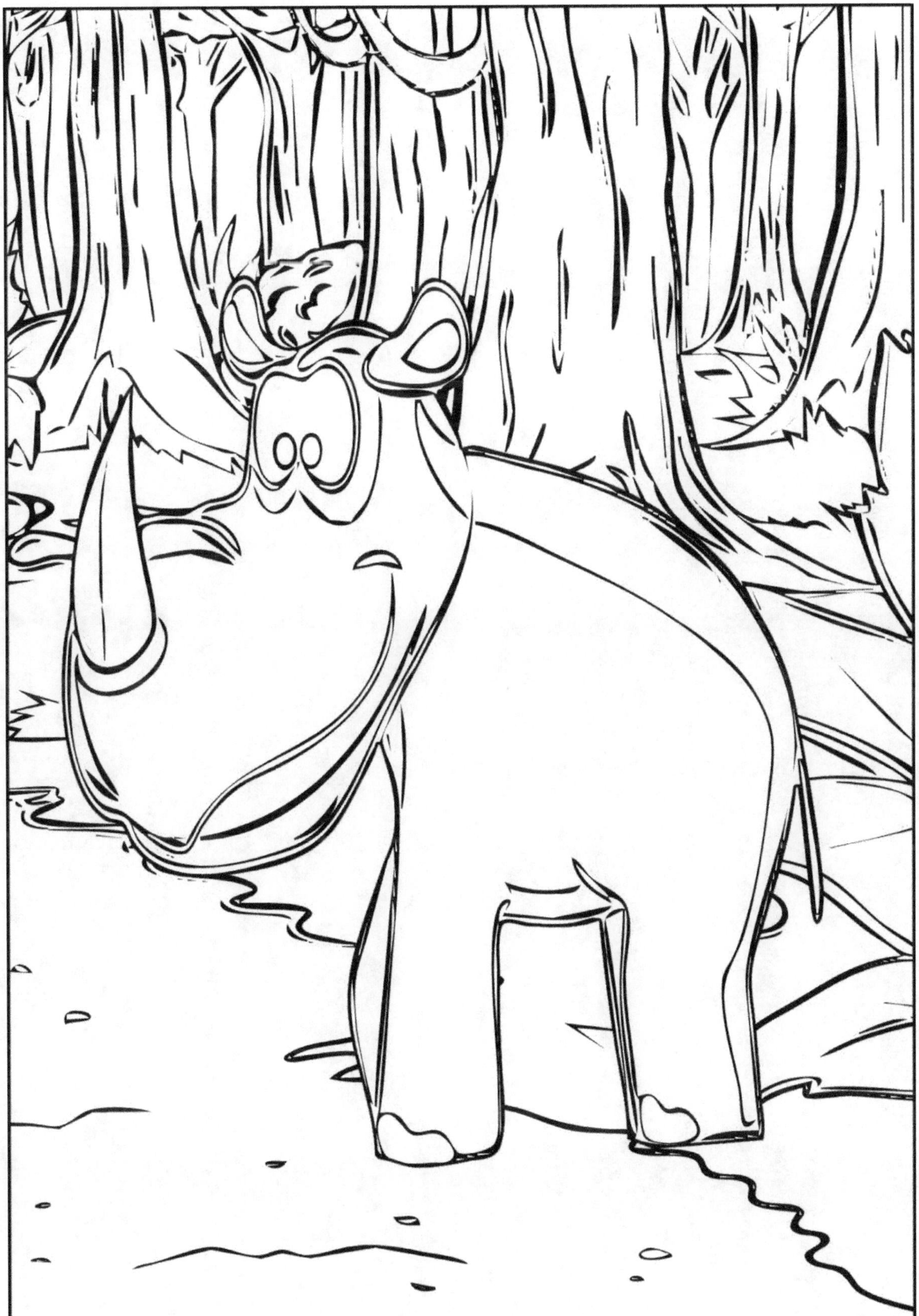

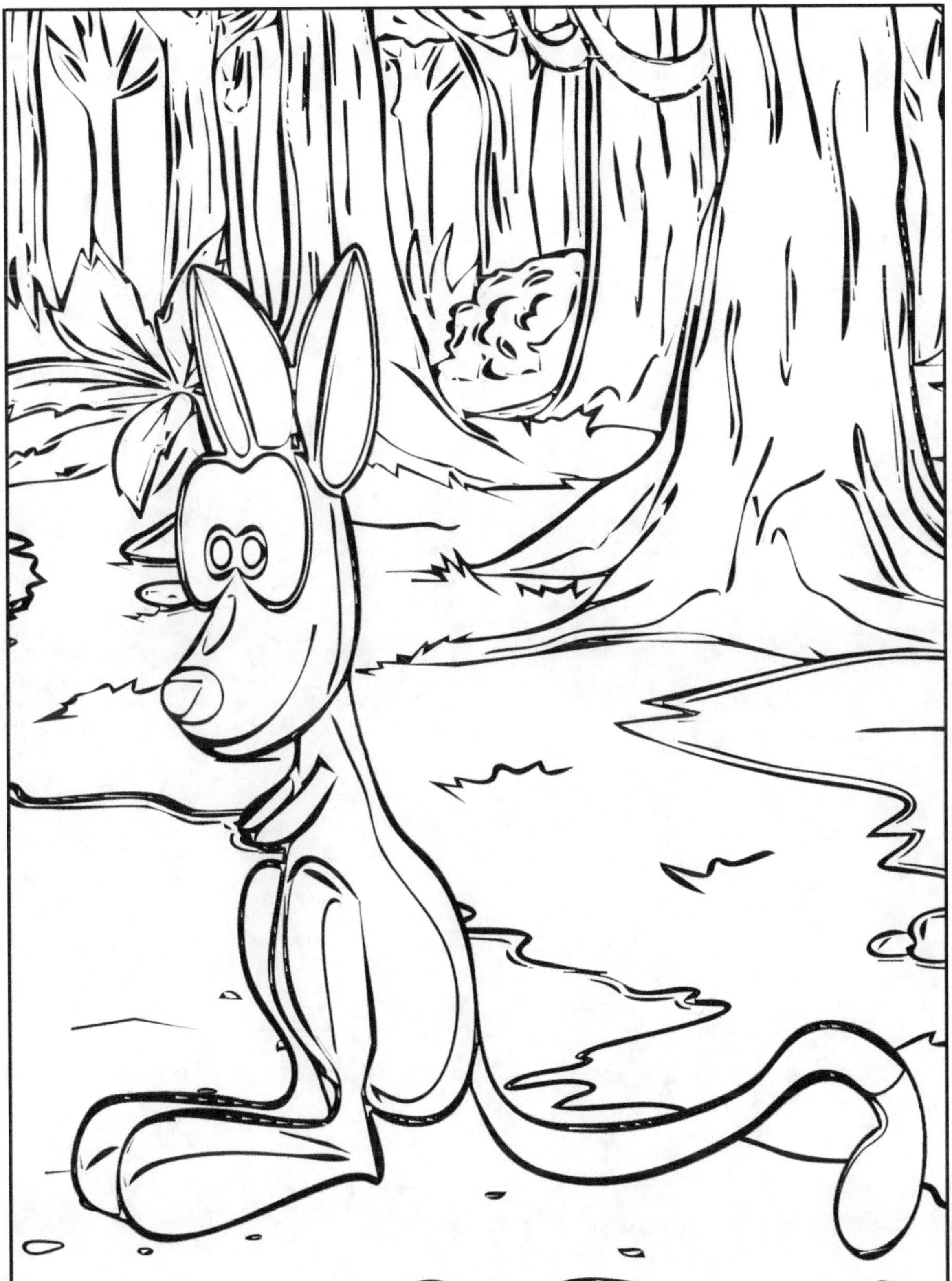

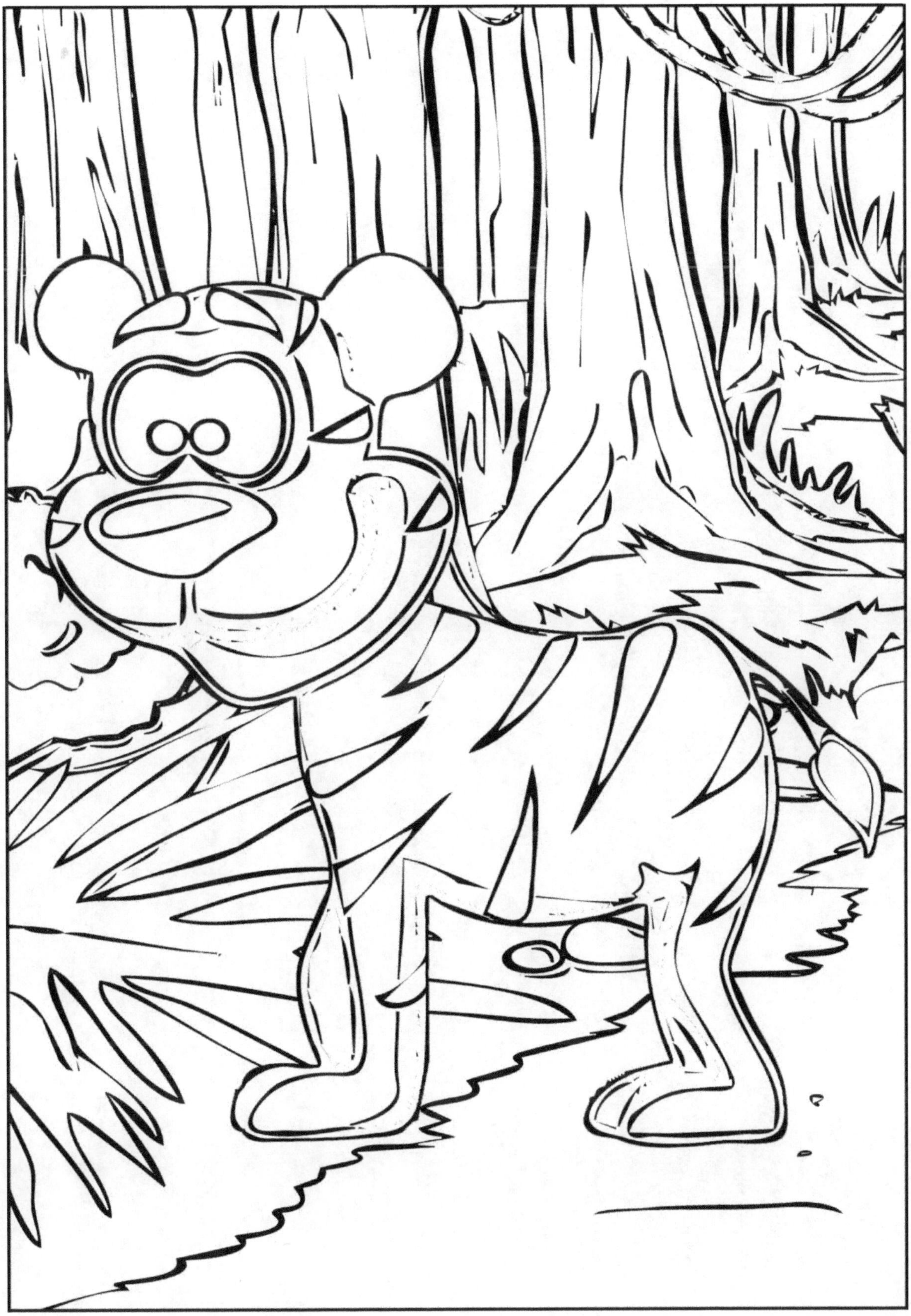

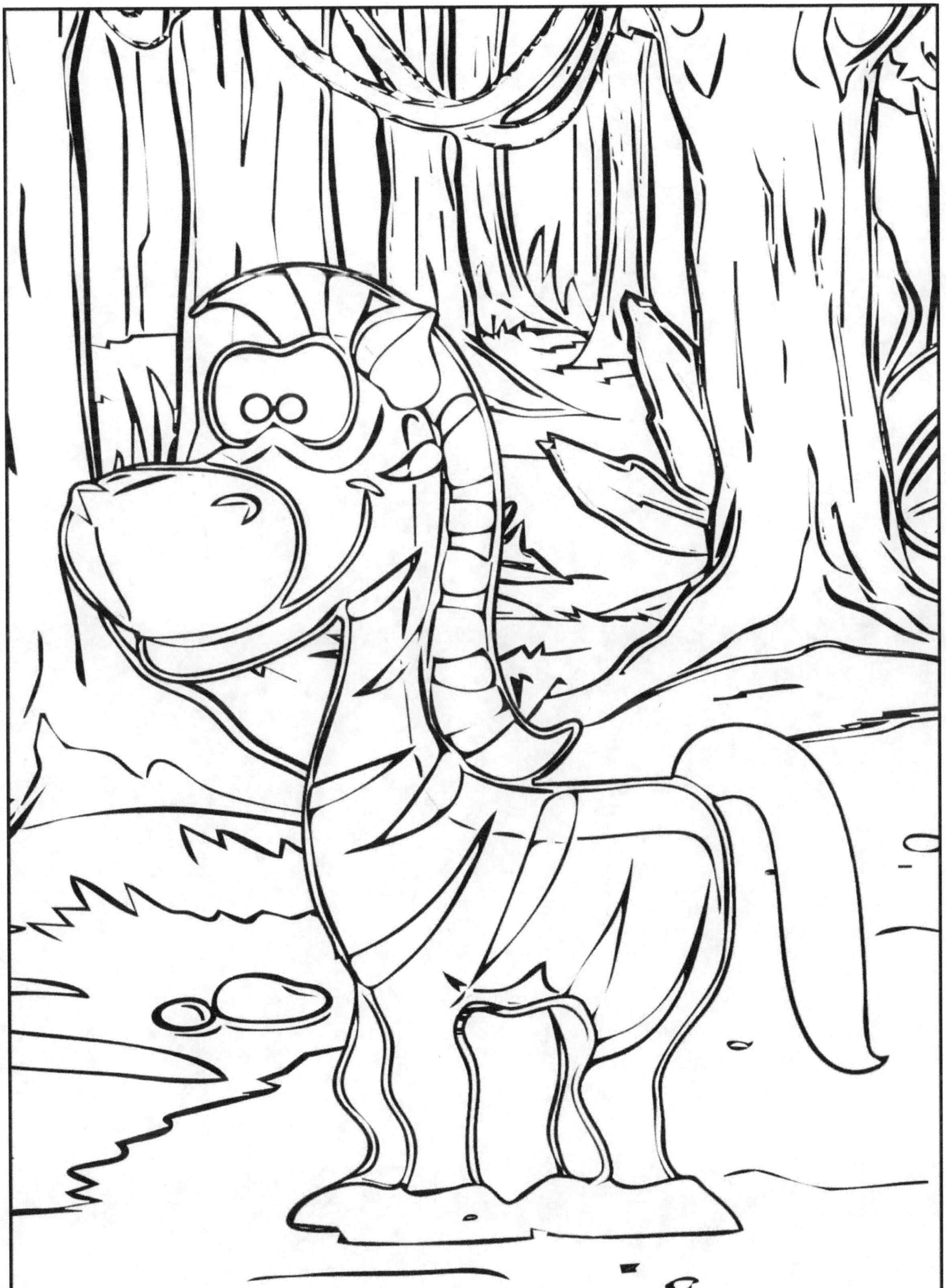

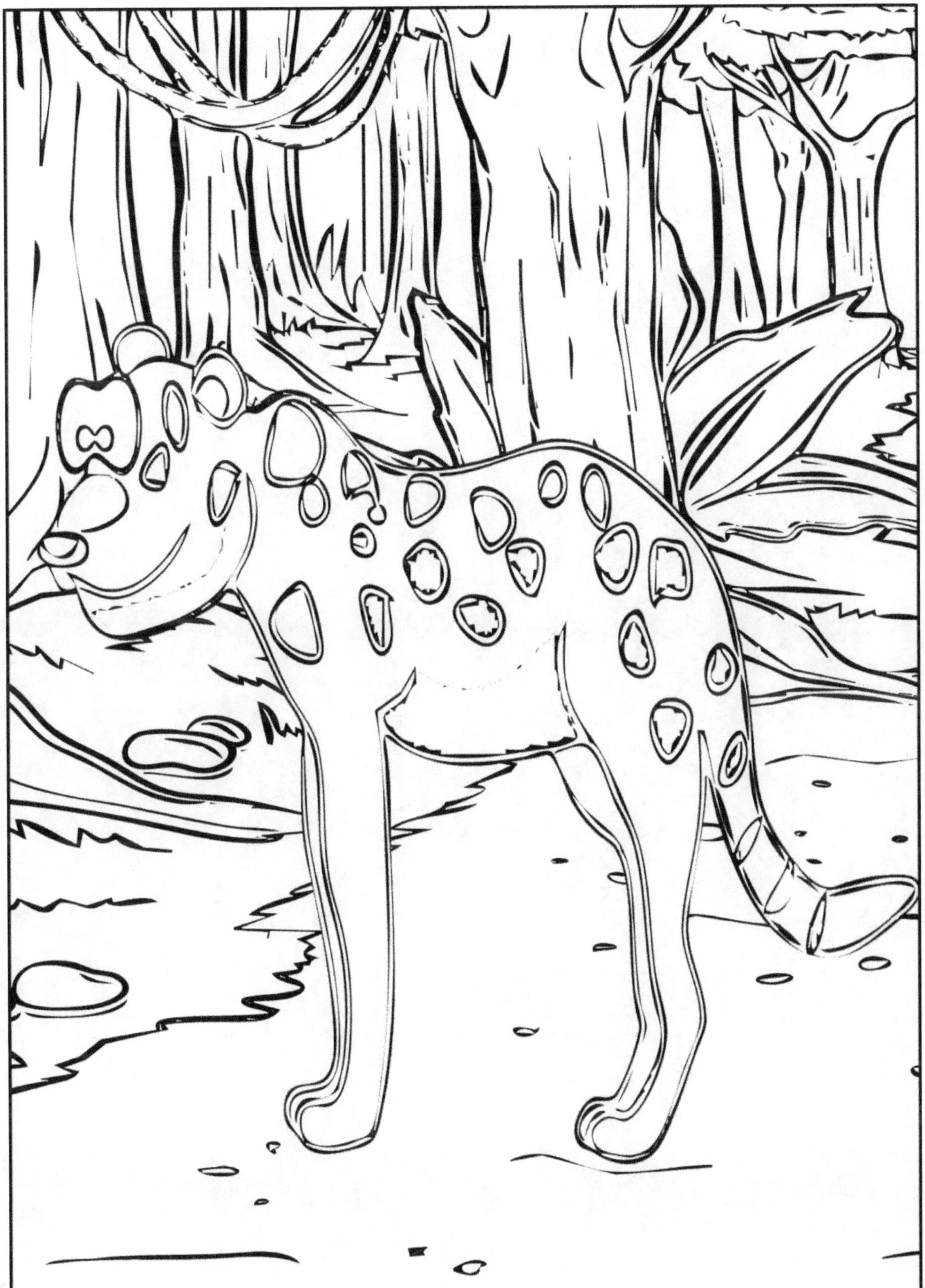

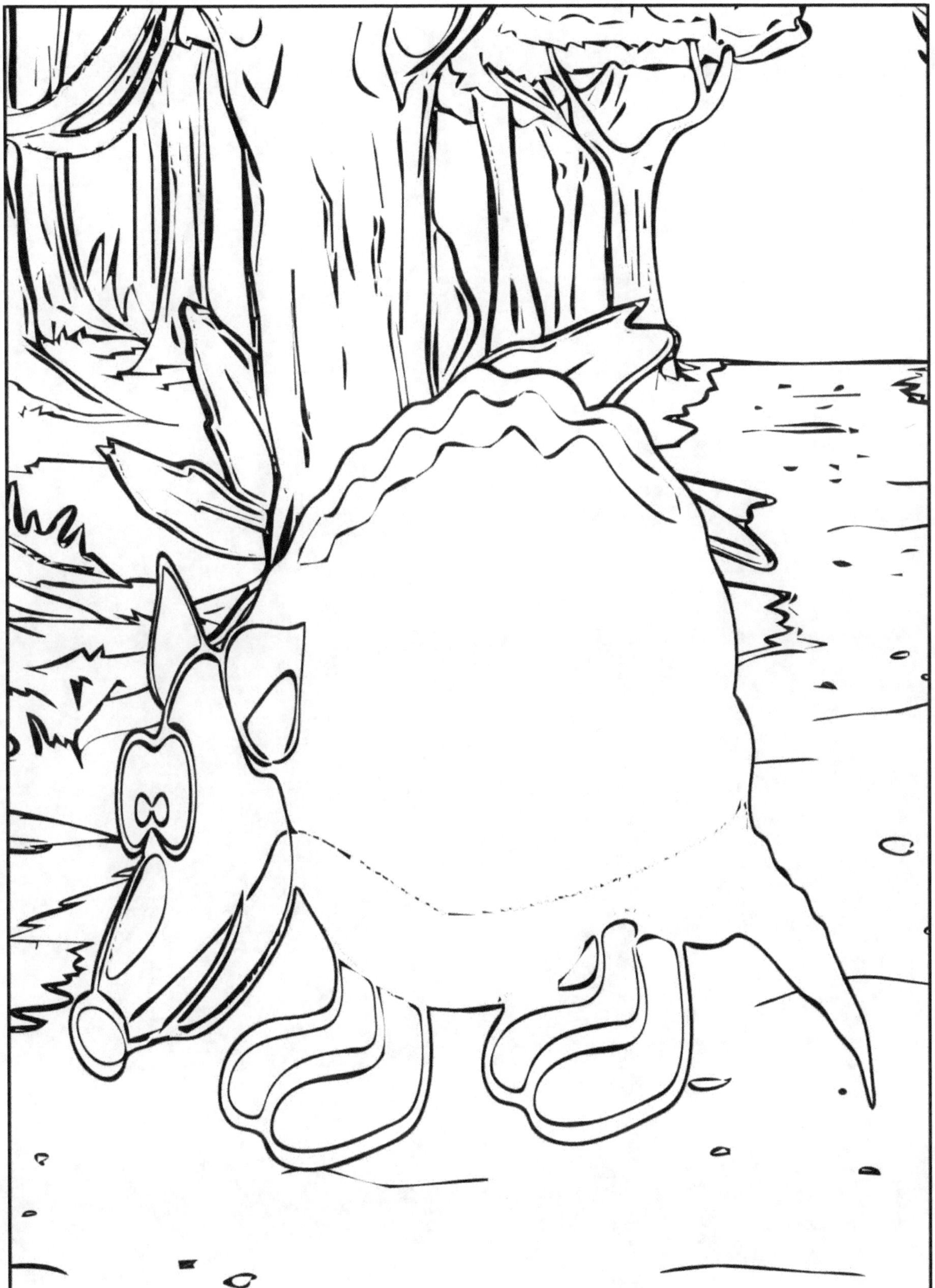

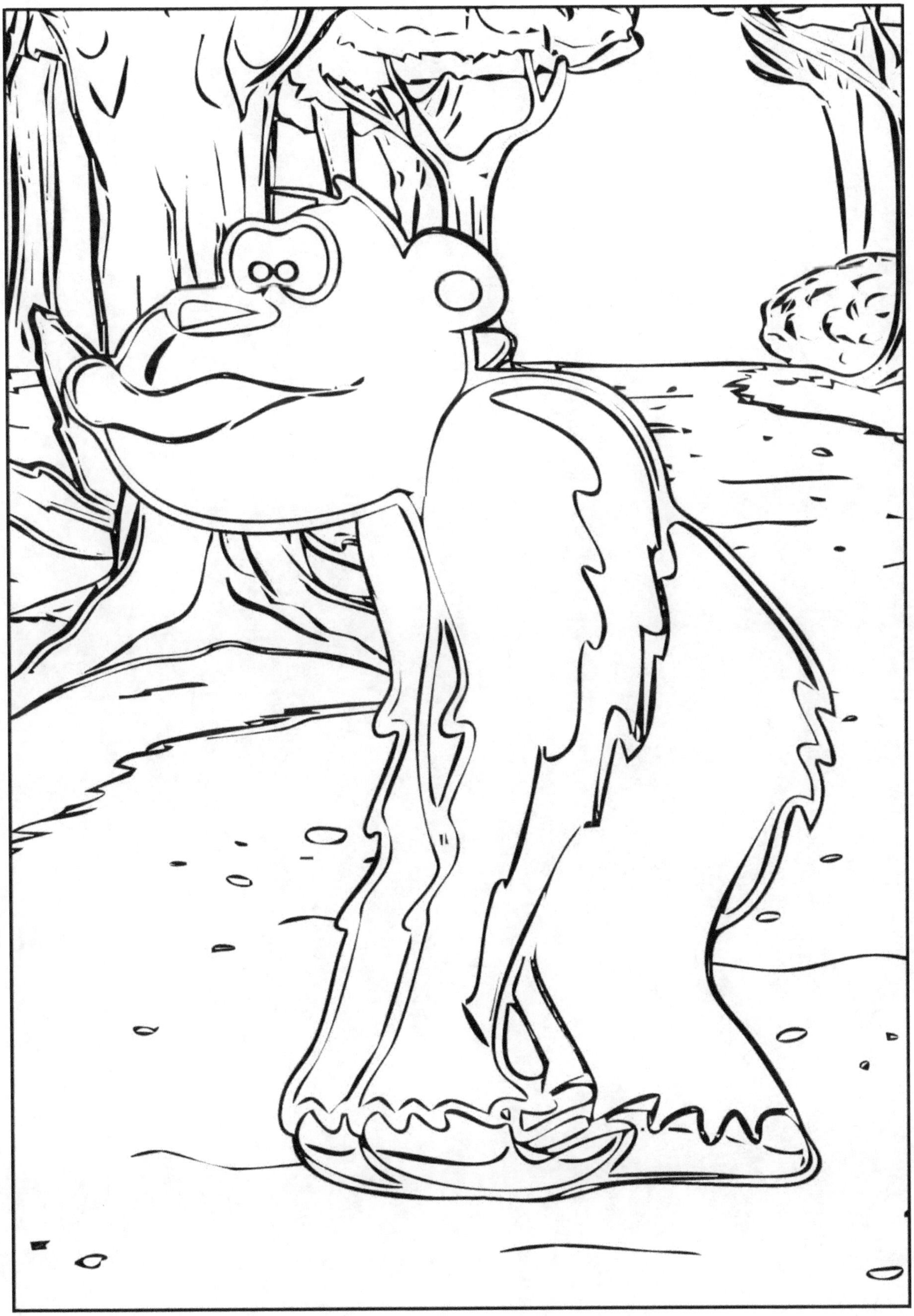

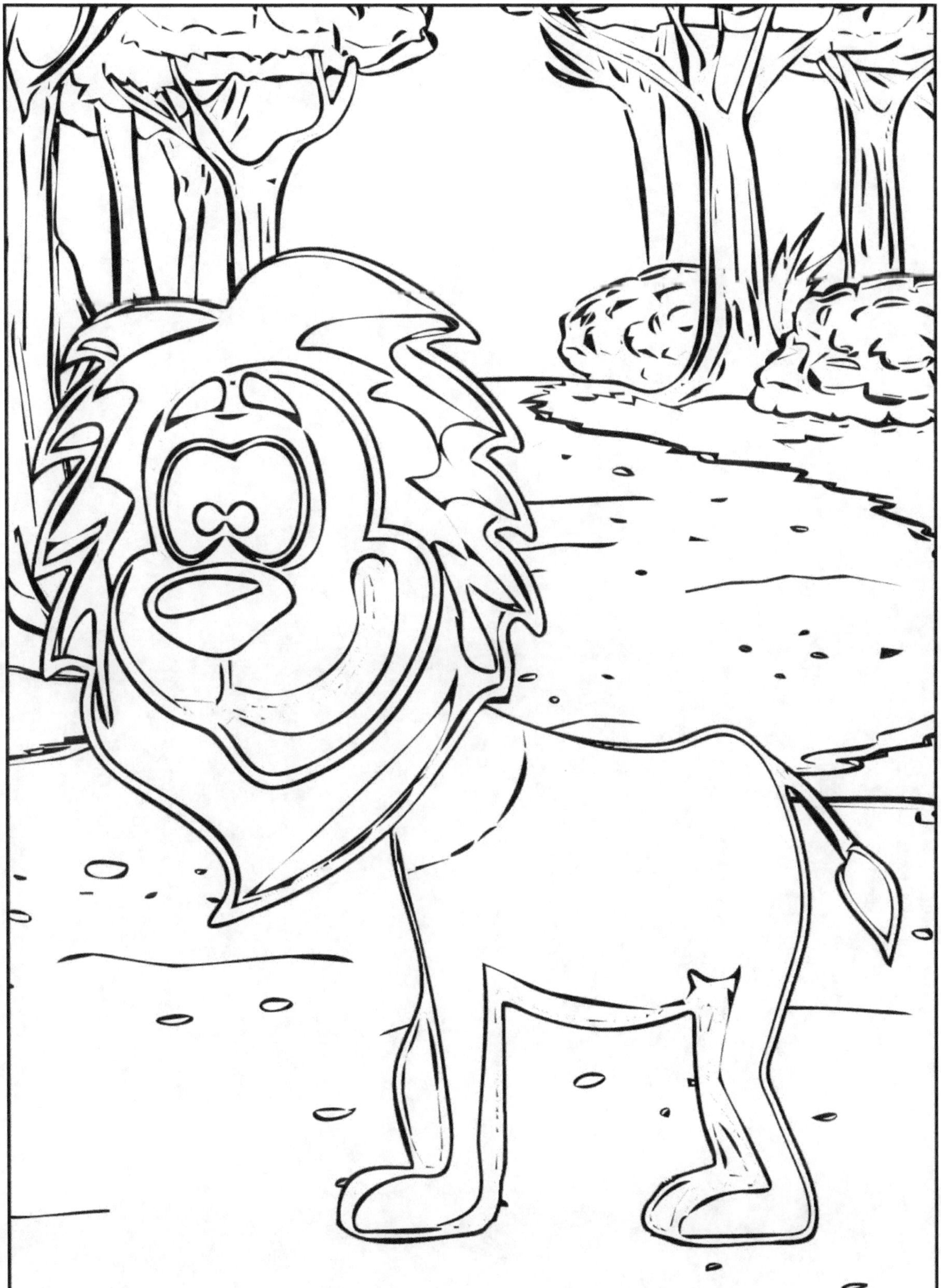

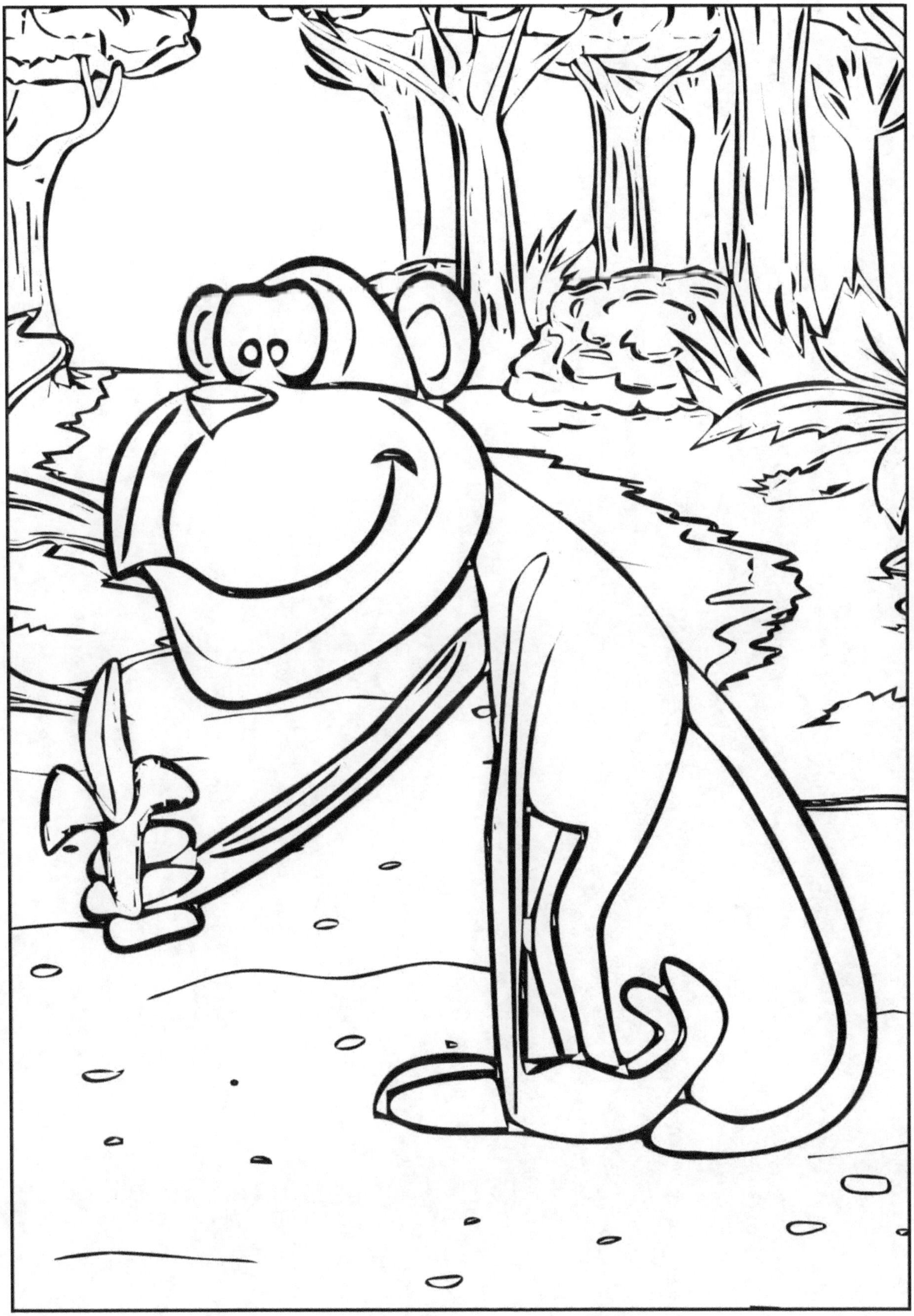

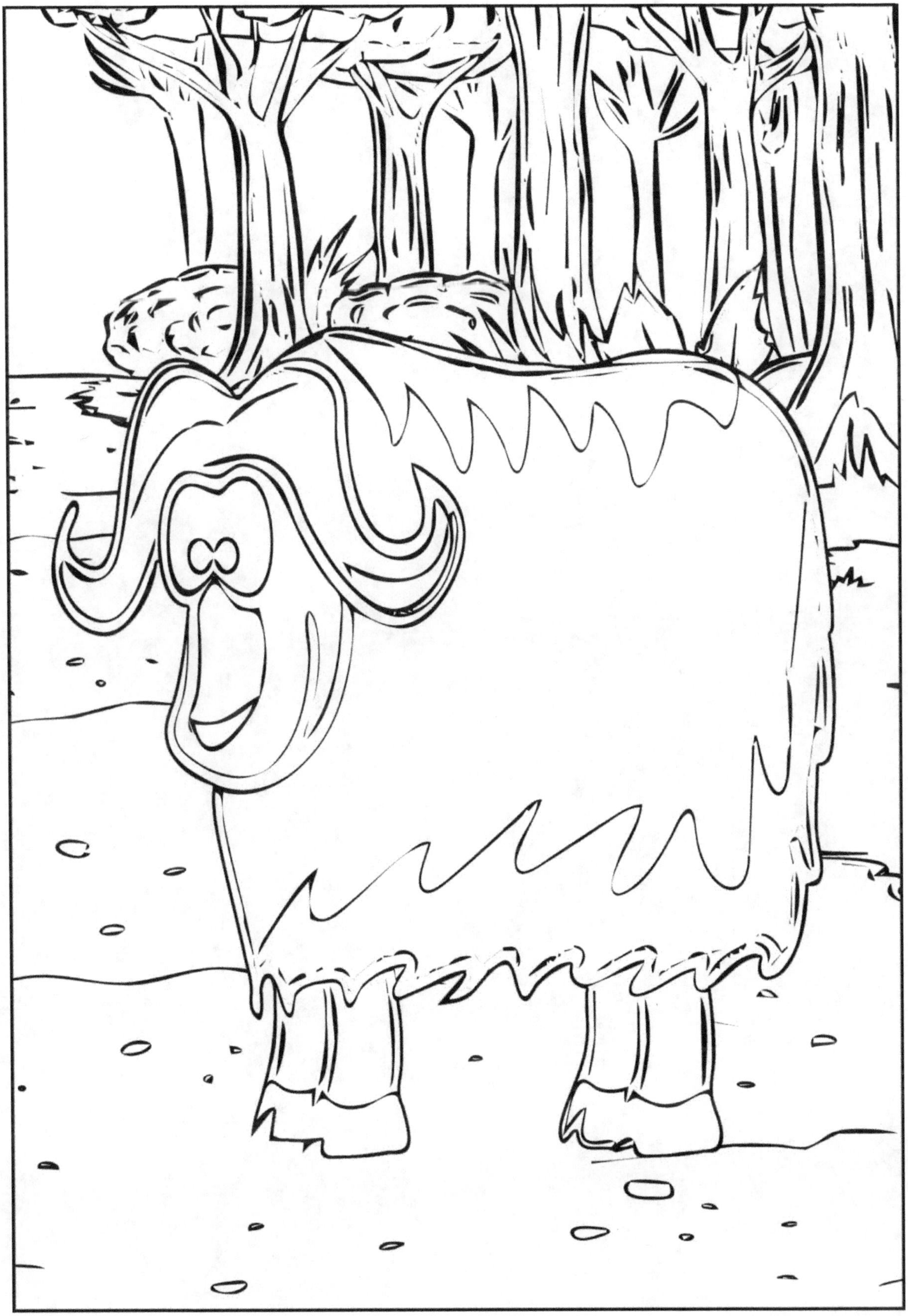

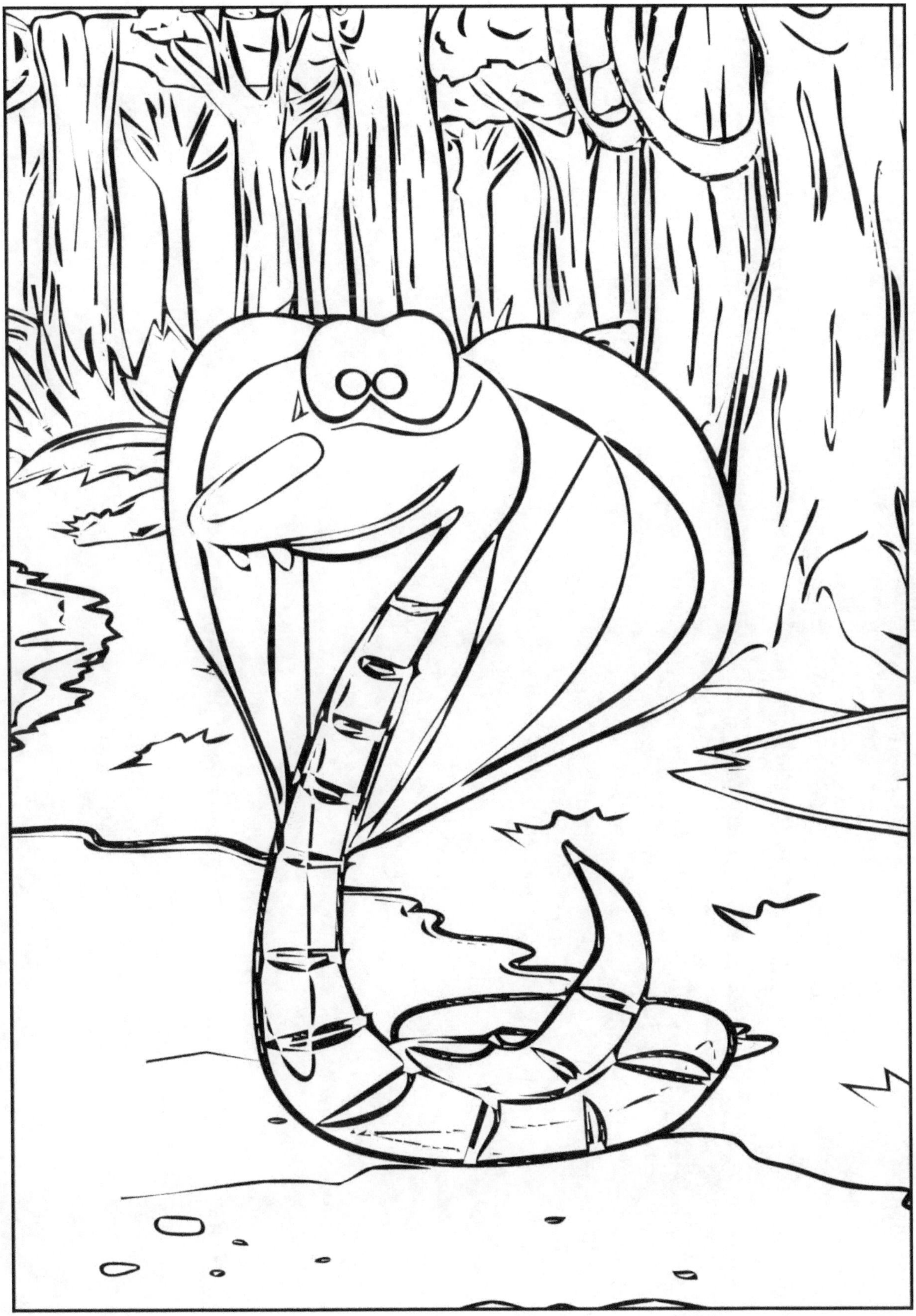

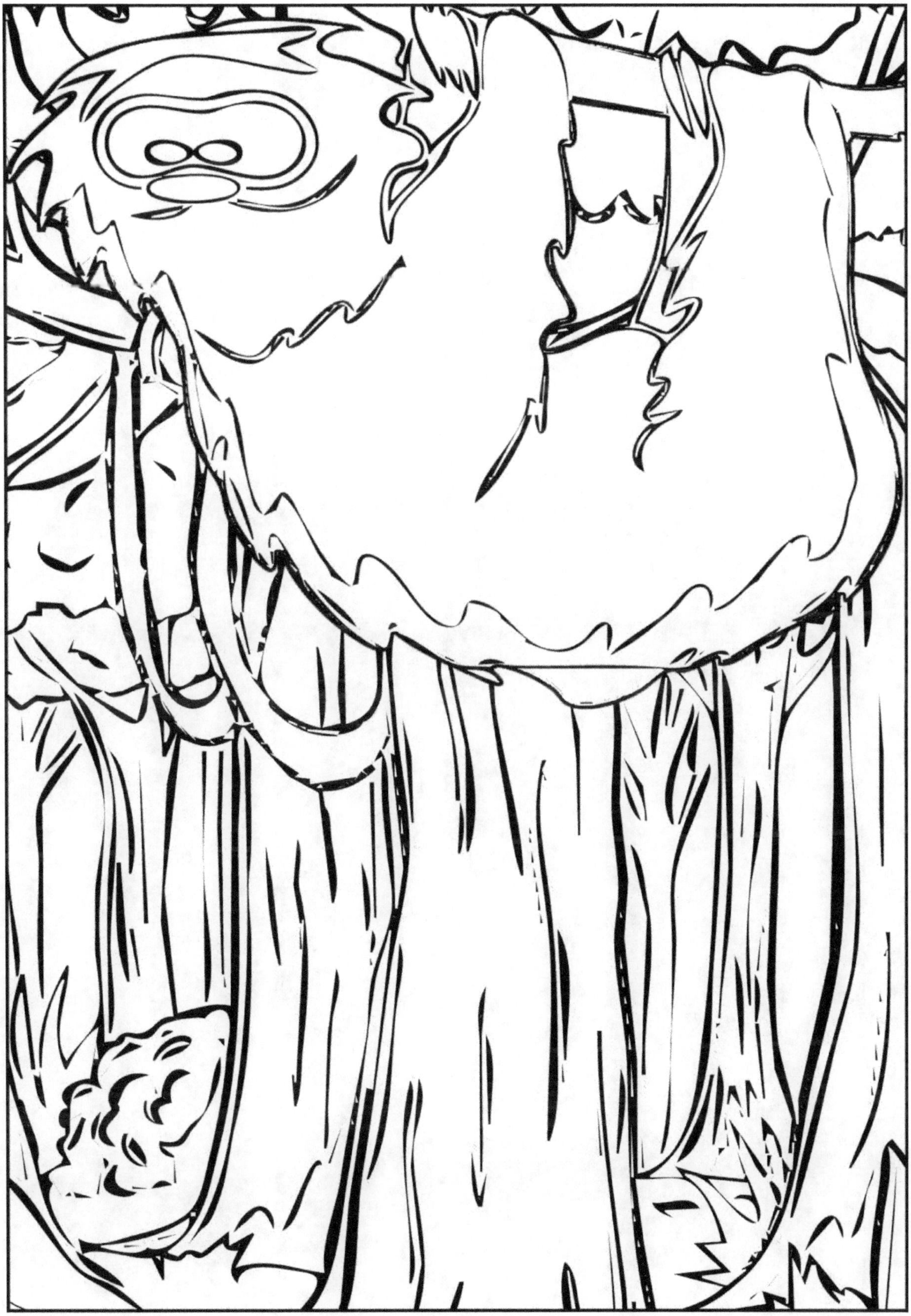

www.ingramcontent.com/pod-product-compliance
Lightning Source LLC
Chambersburg PA
CBHW080609180526
45168CB00007B/2845
9781517498481